HOME FOR SUMMER...
WHAT WILL THEY DO?

Published in 2022
First published in the UK by THP Kidz Zone
An imprint of Tamarind Hill Press Limited
Newton Aycliffe, County Durham, DL5 6XP
Copyright © Rachel Barber
All rights reserved

Email business@tamarindhillpress.com for bulk orders

HOME FOR SUMMER...
WHAT WILL THEY DO?

Rachel Barber

The sun is shining, and the weather is perfect for going outside. That can only mean one thing, it's summer vacation! The kids of Mulberry Lane run outside as fast as they can.

They may be staying home for this summer, but there's still so much fun to be had!

Tommy wants to try out for the soccer team, so he needs to play a lot of soccer to get better. His dad will take him to the park every day, and together they'll play games and practice. Tommy's dad always tells him when he's getting better, which always makes Tommy feel good.

Do you play any sports over the summer?

Julio and Sara like to invite their friend, Sammy, over to their house. They sit down, get comfy, and read all their favourite books. Reading is a lot more fun when you do it with friends.

Then they like to talk about the things they read. Julio has a mystery book that he is excited about, Sara is learning about all the beautiful fish that live in the ocean, and Sammy likes his book about wizards that cast magic spells.

The kids love talking about their favourite books. What are your favourite books to read?

During the summer, so many kinds on Mulberry Lane get to spend more time with their pets. James takes his dog out for walks, but his dog likes to pull on the leash. Caleb taught his dog how to do tricks. Abbott's pet bunny doesn't do much, so they just hang out. Dan and Fran have a big dog with a lot of fur. And Mia has her pet tortoise that she named Mr. Bubber.

Everyone in Mulberry Lane loves their pets.

Do you have a pet you get to spend more time with over the summer? What do you do?

Lana has always wanted to learn how to bake. Now that she has more time over the summer, she can finally learn how to. She will watch videos online and follow the steps to bake all her favourite foods. Lana has made cookies, bread, pizza, and even cake. Lana wants to keep getting better, and maybe even cook dinner for her family when she gets better.

What's something new you want to try over the summer?

Blain likes to go to the park with his friends so they can play basketball. Everyone always has so much fun when they play. It doesn't matter who wins, everyone remembers to be friendly and have fun.

What is your favourite activity to do with friends over the summer? If it's basketball, maybe you could come play with Blain and his friends.

Daisy has decided to practice hula-hooping so she can do 100 loops in a row! It's a tough goal, but Daisy can already do 77 loops. With a little more practice, she knows she can get to 100 loops soon!

It's good to have a goal to challenge yourself over the summer. What's one thing you want to achieve?

Hamish and Paul got new remote-control cars that they like to drive around and race. They started getting bored with their cars, but Hamish had a new idea! He made a game where the cars are playing tag and they have to catch each other.

Have you gotten any new toys or games to play with over the summer? Is there a new game you could play with these toys?

There's so much to do in the summer before school starts again. Even if you spend the whole summer at home, like the kids on Mulberry Lane, there are so many things to do and try! Remember to have fun, and make this the best summer you can!

www.ingramcontent.com/pod-product-compliance
Lightning Source LLC
Chambersburg PA
CBHW081400080526

44588CB00016B/2563